ATTRACT EVERYTHING YOU DESIRE ITS THAT EASY

5 Steps To Reach Abundance Leaving Behind Procrastination, Fear, Doubt, Overwhelm

VINTI BHARATI

I dedicate this book to

My Almighty!

My divine!

Contents

ACKNOWLEDGEMENT

This book is dedicated to the extraordinary mentors who have profoundly transformed my life. Their wisdom has been a guiding light, helping me harness my strengths and fueling my journey with inspiration, encouragement, and unwavering motivation.

A heartfelt thanks goes to my family, whose steadfast support and belief in me have been the bedrock of my achievements. Without their love and encouragement, reaching this milestone would have been a distant dream.

I am also deeply grateful to the Almighty for illuminating my path and for being a constant source of guidance and support.

Happy reading!

INTENTION SETTING: INTRODUCTION

You didn't pick up this book by accident—something within you is ready to unlock the magic that's been waiting to unfold. Before we embark on this transformative journey, let's recognize that every page is filled with wisdom grounded in science, research, and real-life application. This book is more than just words; it's a roadmap to shifting your mindset, empowering you to take control of your life, and training your mind to manifest the life you've always dreamed of.

Imagine breaking free from the thought patterns that have held you back—those invisible barriers that disrupt your peace, health, wealth, and relationships. Now, picture yourself living a life of abundance, where happiness, well-being, and prosperity flow naturally to you.

Ask yourself: Are you ready to embrace a life overflowing with abundance, radiant health, and profound happiness? Do you long for emotional stability and the power to attract the outcomes you've been yearning for?

If so, get ready—this book is about to ignite a transformation that will touch every corner of your life. Are you ready to step into your power and make your dreams a reality? The journey begins now.

We live in a world where information is readily available, and with it comes a deep-seated curiosity to make things happen. I was once where you are now, and then something shifted, transforming my entire life.

As we embark on this journey together, imagine shedding all your old thoughts. You have a fresh

start, filled with new ideas and a renewed sense of self. Allow yourself to focus solely on the future.

We all have dreams, but many of us have buried them while living on autopilot. But what if the universe told you that today is your day to create a new life? What would your desires be? Think about what you want to DO, BE, or HAVE in your life. What do you truly want to achieve, become, or possess? Let abundance be your guiding theme.

You might be wondering what I mean by all this. It all begins with intention. How can you achieve anything without first setting a clear intention?

Imagine asking a travel advisor to plan a trip for you. The first question they'll ask is, "Where do you want to go? For how long? What destinations are on your list?" Designing your life works the same way; you need to know your dreams and desires.

When I took the time to set intentions for my life, I was astonished by the profound desires that surfaced—dreams I had unknowingly buried. Setting a powerful intention allows you to dive deep within yourself. Once you do that, there's no turning back. When you reach out to the universe with unwavering dedication, it responds by guiding you and presenting you with opportunities beyond your imagination.

you want to go? For how long? What destinations are on your list?" Designing your life works the same way; you need to know your dreams and desires.

When I took the time to set intentions for my life, I was astonished by the profound desires that surfaced—dreams I had unknowingly buried. Setting a powerful intention allows you to dive deep within yourself. Once you do that, there's no turning back. When you reach out to the universe with unwavering dedication, it responds by guiding you and presenting you with opportunities beyond your imagination.

Meditation for Intention Setting

This version emphasizes the emotional connection and intention behind the visualization, creating a more immersive and resonant experience.

So Lets' start!!

Before you begin, find a quiet space where you can sit comfortably. Now read the below meditation two times before you start. Put on a relaxing & calming music. Take a deep breath, relax your body, and let your mind become calm. As you settle into stillness, imagine creating a life that fills your heart with joy and fulfilment.

Visualize making choices that align with your highest good. Picture abundance flowing into your life effortlessly. See yourself living in a beautiful home, designed perfectly to your taste. Imagine driving a luxurious car, feeling the smoothness of the ride. Visualize yourself in vibrant health, full of energy and vitality. You are surrounded by love—love from family, friends, and yourself. Envision a life filled with joy, where happiness is a constant companion.

Now, picture yourself on a blissful vacation at a stunning resort, surrounded by the beauty of nature and the warmth of loved ones. You are savouring delicious food, enjoying the luxury of the moment, and feeling deeply connected to your purpose. Your life is driven by meaning and intention, a life where your dreams are manifesting into reality.

Allow your heart to expand with these visions, feeling the warmth of your desires as they take shape. Stay in this space, embracing every detail of the life you are creating. When you feel ready, gently open your eyes with a smile on your face, *knowing that you hold the power to bring these desires into your reality.*

Now, take some time to write down what you truly want to experience in your life. Let your intentions flow from your heart onto the page.

My life stands as the most significant example of the self-realization of the intentions, I once only dreamed of achieving.

It was 2017, and I was on a trip with friends in Jaipur. While everyone around me was having a good time, I felt lost. Despite my smiles and laughter, there was a deep emptiness within me.

When I returned home, I retreated into the comfort of my blanket, isolating myself from everyone. I didn't want to talk, socialize, or connect.

From the outside, everything in my life seemed perfect—a beautiful home, a loving husband, a supportive family. Anyone would have thought I had it all. But no one could see the frustration I felt inside, the void that left me feeling incomplete. I constantly battled with low self-esteem and the nagging belief that I wasn't worthy. Whether real or imagined, it felt like everyone was judging me.

I yearned for my own identity, respect, and a life on my own terms—especially by becoming financially independent. Even the joy of a great weekend or a fun outing was fleeting; something was always missing. I longed for guidance, for someone to show me the way. My loved ones tried to help me find a passion, but I was lost, unsure of what that could be.

Anger, resentment, and frustration clouded my thoughts. When you carry so much negativity within, it colours your entire world. I was living a life of default, taking everything—my health, my relationships, my very existence—for granted. Mornings were spent curled up in bed, mindlessly scrolling through social media, trapped in a comfort zone that was anything but comfortable. Fear and negativity dominated my mind. I used to worry endlessly—about the safety of loved ones when they travelled, about my kids when they came home late, about every little thing. To be honest, I was consumed by worry and insecurity about almost everything.

Toxic relationships surrounded me, filled with gossip, and I was right in the middle of it. I had never thought about earning my own money because life was easy enough, but whenever I wanted something significant, I wished I had my own income, so I didn't have to ask. Financial independence brings a sense of power and self-worth that I craved.

As my children grew older, the loneliness deepened. Eventually, I reached a breaking point. I realized that I couldn't go on like this. Something had to change. The moment I decided to take control of my life, new possibilities began to unfold before me.

My journey had begun!!

I've had some truly transformative journeys—each one a milestone of growth and possibility. As the proud President of WICCI Karnataka, I had the honour of being featured in Femina's Top 8 Women to Inspire in 2022. In 2023, I was recognized as the Social Entrepreneur of the Year by the Women Leaders Forum. I also set the Asia Book of Records for Inspirathon Super Speakers, an initiative with Success Gyan.

Why do I share this? Because if I could achieve this, you absolutely can too. My journey is a testament to what's possible when you believe in yourself, set your intentions, and take that leap.

Your own breakthroughs are waiting—just on the other side of belief.

I DISCOVERED A POWERFUL FORMULA THAT TRANSFORMED MY LIFE, RESHAPED MY WORLD, AND MADE ME A BETTER PERSON. NOW, IT'S TIME TO UNLOCK THIS FORMULA FOR YOU AND IGNITE YOUR OWN TRANSFORMATION.

CHAPTER - 1

UNIVERSE HAS YOUR BACK.

I Always Trust The Direction Of The Universe And Know I'm Being Guided.

Manifestation was a new concept to me. I kept hearing about it but didn't truly understand what it meant. Then, when I felt like life had given up on me, I was introduced to this mysterious power. Intrigued, I began to explore it with relentless curiosity. The more I learned, the deeper my desire grew to understand everything about it.

I decided to apply these principles in my own life, unsure if they would truly work. To my amazement, I began to see real changes. Little by little, my manifestations started to come true. This sparked an even deeper desire to connect with the universe's energy and uncover the secrets behind this magic.

What is this unseen force that billionaires and millionaires' harness to attract abundance? I was determined to find out. With the guidance of my esteemed mentors, I finally discovered the answer. The secret was within me all along. We are all the architects of our destiny.

So, what's the formula? The one that never fails?

It's simple!!

The Highest Energy Wins!

The secret to unlocking the life of your dreams lies in aligning with the highest energy in the UNIVERSE. To manifest a life of beauty and fulfilment, we must first release the patterns and beliefs that no longer serve us. A beautiful life begins with a beautiful mind—one that is clear, intentional, and in harmony with the universe.

Let's dive deeper and explore this powerful truth.

There is energy everywhere and in everything—living things, non-living things. You, me, the people around us. Water, plants, animals—everything. We are vibrating on a frequency all day long. Our mind is the most powerful tool we possess. Medical science has found that every thought reaches every cell of our body. While we can't control external energies, we do have full control over our personal energy.

Researchers have discovered that our mind generates 12,000 to 60,000 thoughts daily, and a staggering 80% of these are negative. That's why things weren't working for me before. I was drowning in negativity and low energy; my vibration was constantly low, and my frequency was perpetually dipped.

We all vibrate at some level or another. Observe your own energy throughout the day. Are you vibrating at a lower frequency or a higher one? Imagine you're trying to tune into a radio station, say 98.3. If you're even a little off from that exact frequency, you won't hear the music you want. The universe operates the same way. Its frequency is always at the highest level, and to align with that, we need to up-level our own energy, our own patterns which no longer serves us.

You want to find the secrets of the universe think in terms of energy, frequency and vibration.

-   Nicola Tesla

The universe doesn't care about our personal desires or needs. It responds to the vibrational energy we emit. If I vibrate at a frequency of fear, guilt, or shame, I will attract experiences aligned with those energies. On the other hand, if I vibrate at a frequency of love, joy, abundance, and happiness, I will attract experiences that match those higher energies. It's that simple. The power is within us.

I remember a time when someone's words would trigger anger and frustration within me, sending my energy into a downward spiral. I would stew in those feelings for hours, unaware of how deeply they were affecting my inner self. My mind was a gateway to negativity, creating emotions that reflected in my outer world, shaping how I reacted and responded to everything.

But then I discovered the science behind manifestation. Just above our spine lies the Reticular Activating System (RAS), a powerful mechanism that filters our thoughts, both positive and negative, throughout the day. The RAS sends this information to our subconscious mind, which then transforms these vibrations into our reality.

When I first grasped this concept, I realized that the universe is constantly vibrating at the highest frequency. But where was I?

Stuck at a low frequency, weighed down by negative thoughts and self-doubt. I knew I had to elevate my energy, to align myself with the higher frequency of what I truly desired.

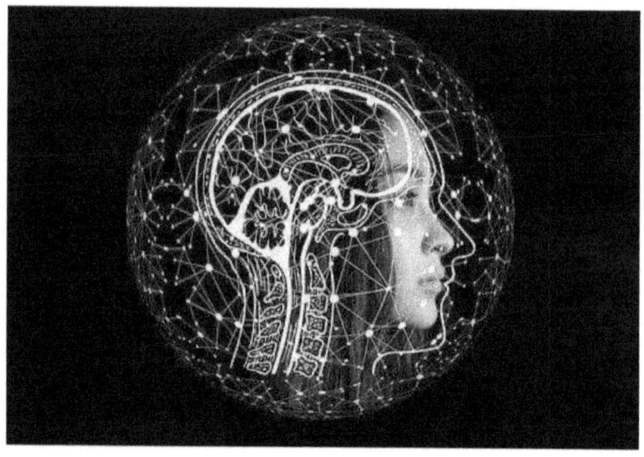

So, I committed to working on my mind. It wasn't easy and took months of consistent effort, but eventually, I unlocked the formula for abundance. By shifting my mindset and using the tools and techniques I had learned, I began to see remarkable results. For instance, I focused on manifesting a specific opportunity that once felt completely out of reach. By consciously raising my energy, visualizing success, and aligning with the universe's frequency, the opportunity came to me almost effortlessly.

As I stayed in this high vibrational energy, magic started to unfold. Even the smallest manifestations began to come to life. I had finally aligned with the universe's frequency, and to my amazement, I had tapped into the true power of the law of attraction.

You might be wondering, "Can I really change and align myself with the frequency of the universe?" It's a valid question, and the journey isn't always easy—but it's absolutely possible.

As I reveal more, I promise to share everything with you. Together, we can change our destiny, refusing to live a life of default.

With each step forward, you'll gain the clarity needed to navigate any situation that arises.

Nothing will hold you back from growing and vibrating at your highest potential.

But first, let's explore what's holding you back. What patterns and essential aspects are preventing you from living the life you truly desire?

CHAPTER- 2

PURPOSE OF CLARITY

Clarity is the moment we see,
Without opening our eyes.

-    *Stephanie Banks*

When I hit a low point in my life and felt like giving up, something deep inside me stirred, urging me to take control. I decided to rebuild myself, exploring every possibility and diving into one course after another, absorbing knowledge and wisdom. Slowly, without even realizing it, my life began to take shape and find its direction.

I realized that the most crucial step is to truly know and love yourself. Your identity defines you, and you cannot live your life wearing someone else's identity. It's not about chasing what others are doing; it's about tuning into your heart and inner voice. That's what I began to do.

After an year of deep reflection, profound realizations, and genuine self-love, my self-worth and self-esteem soared. I started to believe in my abilities again. The first thing I did was to get clear on what I didn't want in my life. When you're clear on what you don't want, the path forward becomes much more straightforward. So, my dear friends, I urge you to write down everything you don't want in your life.

I listed out what I didn't want: fear, resentment, doubt, toxic relationships, procrastination, an unhealthy body, poor eating habits. Once I was clear on what I didn't want, I focused on what I did want—happiness, love, contentment, fulfilment, a healthy body, and positive relationships. As I engaged more with these possibilities, the clarity of my life's direction unfolded.

Now it's your turn, Reflect!!

1. How do you see yourself?

2. What do you truly know about yourself?

KNOWING YOURSELF Are you someone who often falls into the victim mindset? Research shows that those who remain in this mindset prefer the comfort of their comfort zone, even while desiring change. They blame others, complain frequently, and make excuses for their circumstances. Criticism becomes a dominant trait, whether it's at a micro or macro level.

For example, consider someone who constantly criticizes the pollution around them, blaming the government instead of taking action. Why not do your part? Plant a few trees, make a small difference. People who complain and blame stay trapped in victimhood.

Taking ownership of your life is an empowering way to live. Imagine holding the remote control to your life; only you can press play, pause, or rewind. Those who take responsibility and accountability for their lives have a Victor's Mindset. They know how to achieve their goals because they fully own their choices and actions.

Let's create a mantra, inspired by my mentor: *"If it is meant to be, it is up to me."* This life belongs to you. Take 100% responsibility for your choices and mistakes.

Remember, the blame game only lowers your frequency. The goal is to maintain a high vibrational energy. To do that, you must shift from a victim mindset to a victor mindset, taking full ownership of your life.

As Hal Elrod wisely said, *"The moment you take responsibility for everything in your life, is the moment you can change anything in your life."*

❖❖❖

TAKE CHARGE OF YOUR LIFE: E + R = O

Jack Canfield, the renowned author of *Chicken Soup for the Soul*, introduced a powerful formula: E + R = O. It stands for Event + Response = Outcome. In life, we can't always control the events that unfold, but we do have complete control over how we respond—and that response shapes our outcomes.

Let me share an experience. I attended a party where many people complimented me on how radiant I looked. But then, one person came up and remarked, "You look tired. Is everything okay?" Despite all the positive feedback, my mind fixated on that one negative comment. Why did she say that? What did she mean? The event happened, but my response was what determined my evening's outcome.

I had a choice: I could dwell on that single comment and let it ruin my night, or I could focus on the genuine compliments I received and enjoy the evening. I realized that the outcome was entirely in my hands. By shifting my focus, I changed the narrative of the event, which immediately transformed how I felt and acted. I took charge of my mindset, making a conscious decision to stay positive.

This small shift is the first step toward greater consciousness, allowing you to vibrate at a higher frequency and take control of your destiny. Every thought you entertain, whether positive or negative, creates emotions that the universe picks up on. It's not just the words you speak, but the feelings and energy behind them that shape your reality.

If you frequently say, "I'm depressed," or "I'm angry," you're not just stating facts—you're creating your future. It's okay to feel these emotions, but the key is learning to bounce back quickly to a more elevated state. Your goals are important, and to achieve them, you must learn to vibrate at your highest frequency. Remember, in this game of life, THE HIGHEST ENERGY ALWAYS WINS.

In this book, I'll share methods to help you rewire your mindset at every level, empowering you to take charge of your life.

REALIZING TRUE HAPPINESS: SECONDARY & PRIMARY

We often chase after fleeting moments of happiness—a cup of aromatic coffee, a beautiful day, or a joyful outing with loved ones. These experiences can certainly lift our spirits, but they are what I call "secondary happiness." I used to find contentment in these moments, but deep down, I knew something was missing.

I began to question: What is that elusive element that can truly fulfill my soul? I realized that the real purpose of my life was hidden deep within me, waiting to be discovered.

So, I embarked on a journey inward and found what I now call my "primary happiness." This is the kind of happiness that comes from living in alignment with your true passion and purpose—a unique talent or drive that gives meaning to your days and propels you to be the best version of yourself.

If you're feeling lost, it's okay. Your purpose is within you, waiting to be uncovered. Finding it requires patience and self-reflection, but once you do, nurturing and pursuing it daily will bring unparalleled meaning to your life.

For me, this meant letting go of superficial joys and focusing on what truly matters. I discovered my passion for mentoring others on their personal growth journeys. It began when I helped a friend navigate a challenging time in their life, and I realized how much fulfillment I gained from seeing them overcome their struggles. This small act sparked something within me, and I started dedicating more time to guiding others, eventually making it a central part of my life. It wasn't easy, and it didn't happen overnight, but the journey was worth every step, and it transformed my life.

So, relax. Enjoy the process. True happiness is not just about the destination but the journey of discovering and living your passion every day.

For me, this meant letting go of superficial joys and focusing on what truly matters.

Finding Your Dharma: Your Purpose

Simplicity and attention to detail can guide you in discovering your true self. Ask yourself, what truly attracts you? Identify three things you love doing, then seek feedback from family and friends on your strengths and weaknesses. This self-exploration can reveal aspects of yourself that you may overlook but are evident to others.

When I was searching for my passion, I explored various options. My loved ones pointed out that I'm a good listener and often provide practical solutions that benefit them. As I connected these dots, I realized I was drawn to coaching and helping others design and reinvent their lives. This journey has brought me immense fulfillment, knowing that I've helped thousands live the lives of their dreams.

Life isn't just about what happens to us—it's about how we aspire to shape it. Start by identifying your skill sets. List three things you're good at, then consider what you value most and what brings you joy. For example, if you love cooking and enjoy interacting with people, you could combine these passions by creating cooking videos or offering online cooking classes.

Another Example: Imagine someone who loves gardening and enjoys teaching others. They realize that these two passions can be combined into a purpose. They start a community garden and offer workshops on sustainable gardening practices. This not only brings them joy but also fulfills their purpose of educating others and contributing to the community. By aligning their skills and passions, they live a life of purpose and abundance.

This is how you can merge your skills and passions to find your purpose.

Pay close attention to your patterns—what do you spend most of your time on? Who do you admire? What content do you gravitate towards on YouTube or social media? To deepen your self-understanding, dedicate 30 minutes each day to calm reflection or meditation.

Here's a meditation practice to help you start:

Meditation for Finding Purpose

Find a comfortable position, relax your body, and calm your mind. When you're fully relaxed, visualize yourself creating a beautiful life. See yourself helping others, living a goal-driven and purposeful life. Imagine the fulfilment that comes from enriching others' lives, and feel your heart expand as you envision abundance and support from the universe. When you feel complete, gently open your eyes with a smile.

This meditation can help you think more expansively about your life. Just as artists create in moments of calm, you can create your life with intention. Regularly ask yourself these four questions:

1. What do you want from your life?

2. What experiences do you want to have?

3. How do you want to grow from these experiences?

4. How will you use this growth to serve the world?

Your answers will guide you to your dharma.

Let's take full responsibility for our lives—move beyond complaining, blaming, and making excuses. Shift from asking ***"Why me, God?"*** to *"How can I?"* Remember, the mantra for our lives should be: ***"If it is meant to be, it is up to me."***

If you're still figuring out your biggest goal, start with a theme of abundance. Focus on this goal, and whenever your mind wanders, realign yourself with the universal energy that helps you manifest abundance. The law of attraction works when you vibrate at the highest frequency, matching that of the universe. When you elevate your mindset to match empowering emotions, life will begin to work in your favor.

One of the simplest ways to shift your mindset is through gratitude. We often focus on what we lack, but by concentrating on what we already have, we can change our life's narrative. When you stay in gratitude, your conscious mind signals to your subconscious that you are blessed and receiving the best. This opens the door for more blessings to flow into your life. Gratitude is a simple yet powerful tool that helps manifestation work effortlessly.

"The more you practice the art of thankfulness, the more you have to be thankful for."

-   Norman Vincent Peale

◆◆◆

CHAPTER- 3

BELIEFSTHAT HOLD US

Vibrating constantly at the highest level is a challenge. Many factors can hold us back, but one of the most significant barriers to our growth is our belief system. These beliefs can silently limit our potential, becoming invisible intruders that prevent us from succeeding in various aspects of life. Let's explore how these belief systems form and how they can hold us back.

Our belief systems are deeply rooted in the evolution of our brains. The reptilian brain, responsible for survival, focuses on basic needs like eating, drinking, breathing, and sleeping. The limbic brain, where the amygdala resides, governs our emotions and is constantly concerned with one question: "Am I safe?"

To understand how belief systems form, let's go back to the time of our ancestors. They lived in caves, constantly on alert to hunt and protect themselves. Fear was essential for survival, keeping them vigilant and safe. Over generations, this fear was passed down and deeply embedded in our psyche.

As humanity evolved, we began assigning meaning to everything around us, gathering evidence of what was 'right' and 'wrong.' Gradually, these beliefs started to take shape, influenced by society and the people around us. Often formed during our most impressionable years between the ages of 1 and 7, these beliefs are heavily influenced by our parents, friends, and early experiences.

Before my marriage, I worked in a company that handled advertising and marketing. Unhappy in that job, I left, hoping to find something more fulfilling. I took another job, believing it was the right fit, but again, happiness eluded me. My family, with the best intentions, questioned my choices, wanting to ensure I made the 'right' decisions. While their intentions were pure, the impact on me was profound. I began to doubt my ability to make good decisions, and my confidence waned.

After marriage, I made fewer choices for myself. The fear of making the 'wrong' decision became so ingrained that it paralyzed me. Every time I faced a choice, I felt dread, convinced that whatever I chose would lead to failure. This limiting belief held me back, causing me to retreat into my comfort zone, living a life that didn't feel like my own.

I had created patterns that were not serving me well—habits of thinking, feeling, and acting that shaped my life. Even when a great opportunity came my way, I would push it aside, influenced by the negative patterns I had built. When these patterns are positive, they can propel us toward our goals and dreams. But when they are rooted in negative beliefs, they can become chains that bind us, keeping us from reaching our true potential.

For much of my life, I was trapped in a cycle of self-doubt and low self-worth. I believed that I could not achieve anything significant, that I was not deserving of success or happiness. This pattern was so deeply ingrained that it became my reality. I would look at others who were successful and think, "That could never be me." I convinced myself that I wasn't smart enough, talented enough, or worthy enough to pursue my dreams.

I had never earned money, reinforcing my belief that I was a failure. I felt as though I had nothing to offer—no skills, no talents, no value. This destructive pattern of thinking consumed me, and I began to internalize these beliefs. I started to believe that this was my fate, that I was destined to live a life of mediocrity, always struggling, always falling short.

These destructive patterns didn't just affect my thoughts; they affected every aspect of my life. I became afraid to take risks or try new things because I was convinced, I would fail. I stayed in my comfort zone—a place of fear and self-imposed limitations. I constantly second-guessed myself, doubted my abilities, and felt unworthy of any success or happiness.

This pattern of thinking kept me from pursuing opportunities that could have changed my life. I missed out on chances to grow, learn, and achieve because I was too afraid to step out of the shadows of my self-doubt. My life became a series of missed opportunities and unfulfilled potential, all because I allowed these destructive patterns to dictate my actions.

Breaking Free from Destructive Patterns

The turning point came when I realized that these patterns were not facts but beliefs—stories I had been telling myself for years, based not on truth but on fear. I began to understand that I had the power to change these patterns, to rewrite the story of my life.

It wasn't easy. Breaking free from destructive patterns requires a conscious effort to challenge and change the beliefs that have been holding you back. It involves identifying the negative thoughts and behaviours that are keeping you stuck and replacing them with positive, empowering ones.

For me, this process started with small steps. I began to question my beliefs about myself and my abilities. For instance, I used to believe that I wasn't good at public speaking. The thought of speaking in front of a group terrified me, and I avoided it at all costs. But I knew that if I wanted to grow, I had to face this fear.

So, I started small. I volunteered to speak at a local community meeting—just a short introduction, nothing too overwhelming. My heart was racing, and my mind was filled with doubts, but I pushed through. Afterward, I realized it wasn't as terrifying as I had imagined. The more I did it, the more confident I became. Over time, what once seemed impossible became something I could do with ease.

This small step helped me challenge my belief that I wasn't a good speaker. It taught me that my fears were just stories I was telling myself, not facts. By gradually stepping out of my comfort zone, I began to rewrite the narrative about what I was capable of.

I took small risks, stepped out of my comfort zone, and proved to myself that I was capable of more than I had ever imagined. Slowly but surely, I began to build confidence in myself and my abilities. I started to believe that I was worthy of

success, that I had something valuable to offer, and that I could achieve my dreams.

Shifting Beliefs with FSFA (Facts, Story, Feeling, Action)

One of the powerful tools that changed my life was FSFA—Facts, Story, Feeling, Action. It helps shift limiting beliefs by transforming the story you tell yourself.

Example:

- FACT: I am not earning enough money.

- STORY: I never have enough for anything.

- FEELING: I feel pathetic and low.

- ACTION: I sulk and stay in a negative headspace.

By changing the story, everything changes:

- FACT: I am not earning enough money. (Fact remains same)

- STORY: I have everything I need by God's grace. Let me explore new directions to improve my situation.

- FEELING: I feel excited to explore new possibilities.

- ACTION: I am energized and ready to restart my journey.

Remember, your life transforms when you set the right beliefs. Whatever has been holding you back for years, recognize it, and shift it. By improving your vibrational frequency, you can

achieve all the results you desire. As I've said before, it's a game of energy—the HIGHEST ENERGY ALWAYS WINS. With the right mindset and beliefs, you can elevate your life to new heights.

Within you is the power to do things you never dreamed possible. this power becomes available to you just as soon as you change your beliefs.

-     Maxwell Maltz

CHAPTER 4

KNOWING OUR ENEMY-YOUR RESISTANCE

Life Is Staying Beyond Fear and Doubt.

Battling Resistance—The Ravana Within

Whenever I set out to achieve something significant, resistance would emerge in full force. It's as if an unseen enemy knew me better than I knew myself. This enemy, which I've named Ravana, is relentless. It's invisible, cunning, and consistently destructive. It never sleeps, always waiting to strike when I'm most vulnerable.

Resistance is that voice in your head that tells you to hit the snooze button instead of waking up early to pursue your goals. It's the force that causes your car to break down just when you're about to give an important presentation or makes you miss a flight on the day of a crucial meeting. Ravana knows exactly when to intervene to keep you from crossing the finish line.

By naming this enemy Ravana, I could better understand and confront it. Knowing your Ravana is key to recognizing when it arrives, so you can prepare to shut it down. Our life's purpose is to live fully, but Ravana's mission is to pull us back.

Fear and Doubt: The Twin Heads of Ravana

Fear and doubt were Ravana's most potent weapons. For example, when I first decided to take control of my life, I was filled with fear and self-doubt. I was stepping into the unknown, leaving behind a life that was familiar but unfulfilling. Every time I tried to move forward; I questioned my capabilities. I felt insecure and constantly worried about how others would perceive me. This fear was particularly strong when I was about to speak publicly or make a critical decision in my business. The fear of failure and judgment would paralyze me, making me want to retreat.

But I learned to have a conversation with my Ravana, telling it to stay out of my sight, confined to a corner of my mind where it couldn't interfere with my dreams. Although Ravana often tried to interrupt, I refused to listen. I reminded myself of the times I had succeeded despite my fears, like when I stepped up as the President of WICCI Karnataka and led initiatives that were recognized on a national level. The more I confronted Ravana, the stronger I became, and each victory over fear and doubt added to my confidence.

Procrastination: The Lure of Delay

Ravana also manifested as procrastination, especially when I was just starting to build my dream life. I remember the early days of my entrepreneurial journey when everything seemed overwhelming. I was trying to establish my identity, create a successful business, and balance personal responsibilities all at once. The sheer volume of tasks often led me to delay starting on the most important ones. I wasn't clear about where I was headed, and this lack of clarity led to delays.

Understanding procrastination was crucial in helping me overcome it. I discovered that I often procrastinated because I was unsure about my direction or lacked confidence in my abilities. I would delay important tasks, telling myself I would get to them later, but later often turned into never.

To combat this, I used Mel Robbins' 5-Second Rule. Whenever I felt the urge to procrastinate, I would count down from five—5, 4, 3, 2, 1—and then immediately start on the task. This simple practice prevented resistance from creeping back in. I also began using the 2-Minute Rule, which meant starting tasks I was dreading for just two minutes. More often, than not, once I started, I found the momentum to keep going.

I also realized that my procrastination stemmed from a lack of clarity. To address this, I took time to define my goals and break them down into smaller, actionable steps. This way, the tasks seemed less overwhelming, and I could tackle them one at a time.

Overwhelm: The Weight of Ambition

Overwhelm was one of Ravana's most effective tactics against me. I remember when I first started working on a major project—launching a new business initiative. The end goal was enormous, and the number of tasks involved was daunting. I would sit down to work, only to feel paralyzed by the sheer scale of what needed to be done. There were so many moving parts, and the big question in front of me was how to start and where to begin.

To overcome this, I learned the art of dumping everything down on paper. I would list all the tasks that needed to be done and then prioritize them by marking each one as Easy, Medium, or Hard. By chunking my work into manageable pieces, I could tackle one step at a time, reducing the overwhelm and maintaining momentum. For example, when I was working on organizing a large-scale event, I started by breaking down the tasks into daily to-dos, from contacting speakers to coordinating with vendors. This method allowed me to focus on one thing at a time, gradually building up to the event day without feeling overwhelmed.

Imbalance: The Struggle for Harmony

Ravana would also throw me off balance, leading to feelings of guilt. When I was intensely focused on my mission to build a successful coaching practice, I found myself neglecting other aspects of my life, like health and family. There were times when I worked late into the night, missing out on quality time with my loved ones, and neglecting my self-care routine.

I realized that this imbalance, though difficult, was sometimes necessary to achieve my goals. Instead of striving for perfect balance, I aimed for harmony. I accepted that during certain periods, some areas of my life would take a back seat. But I also made sure to compensate later—spending quality time with my family on weekends or making up for missed workouts with more intense sessions when I had the time. For instance, after completing a particularly demanding project, I made it a point to take a short vacation with my family, fully disconnecting from work to recharge and reconnect.

Comparison: The Thief of Joy

Comparison was another form Ravana took to undermine my progress. Watching others succeed made me feel unworthy. I remember the time when I saw my peers achieving milestones in their careers while I was still struggling to establish myself. This comparison made me question my own worth and capabilities. I started to doubt whether I could ever achieve the same level of success.

But I soon realized that those who inspired me had also faced their own struggles. Your journey is unique to you. Instead of comparing, I learned to get inspired by others' achievements. I reminded myself that my path was different, and that success would come in its own time. For instance, when I felt the sting of comparison, I would focus on my own progress, celebrating small wins like completing a successful workshop or receiving positive feedback from a client. Over time, this shift in perspective helped me focus on my journey rather than others.

Ravana was strong, but I was stronger. I reminded myself daily of the immediate actions I needed to take whenever Ravana appeared. Let me share this mantra with you:

There is an enemy. The enemy will destroy me. The enemy is inside me. The real me must fight the resistance in me. My dreams and desires are essential to me. Assistance will follow the minute I overcome my resistance, my Ravana.

Now, I want you to imagine something beautiful. Picture yourself standing on the tallest mountain, with the wind gently blowing and greenery all around. You savor every moment with all your senses. As you approach the cliff's edge, you look down and feel a rush of fear. But then, suddenly, you sprout wings and begin to fly. Fear vanishes, replaced by the exhilaration of soaring through the sky. This is how you'll feel when you step out of your comfort zone and overcome your resistances.

Imagine a life without fear, doubt, or resistance. How much could you achieve? Your dreams and desires are crucial, and your goal of living an abundant life is within reach. You are unique, and you possess the power to manifest your dreams.

Remind yourself often: I need to vibrate at the frequency of the universe by overcoming all my resistances—fear, doubt, procrastination, and more. Every day, I worked on defeating my resistance. Now, I challenge you to do the same. Identify three resistances that overpower you, choose your strategies to overcome them, and commit to winning this battle.

Ask yourself, *"When will I be the master of my mind?"* Or will you allow your mind to be the master of your thoughts?

◆ ◆ ◆

"FOLLOW YOUR DREAMS & DESIRES, BELIEVE IN YOURSELF & DON'T GIVE UP"

CHAPTER 5
TAPPING THE POWER

Never trust your fears; they do not
Know your strengths.
               -      *Athene Singh*

Living a life plagued by distress and negative thoughts was a challenge that did not leave me easily. Yet, my unwavering determination to reclaim my self-identity, respect, and financial independence was the driving force that helped me bounce back. I discovered that nothing could stand between me and my dreams. I learned to elevate my emotions consistently and align with the highest power to manifest my desires.

One of the most profound lessons I learned was the art of shifting my mindset. Rewiring my conscious awareness required dedication and the application of various tools and techniques. I call this

The Art of the Pivot.

Shifting Words, Shifting Energy

One of the most profound lessons I've learned on my journey is the immense power of language—specifically, how the words we choose to speak to ourselves can either drain our energy or uplift it. Our internal dialogue shapes our emotional state, and in turn, our emotional state influences how we experience life. This simple yet transformative realization has the potential to radically change the way you navigate challenges.

Imagine this all-too-common scenario: you're stuck in traffic, and the frustration begins to build. Your mind starts spinning with thoughts like, "These traffic jams are driving me crazy! I can't stand this!" As these negative thoughts take root, you might feel your body tense up, your mood darken, and your stress levels rise. You're not just stuck in traffic—you're stuck in a cycle of negative energy that magnifies the discomfort of the situation.

But here's the truth: while you may not have the power to change the external situation—the traffic, in this case—you absolutely have the power to change your internal response. This is where the art of the pivot comes into play. By consciously choosing to shift from disempowering language to empowering language, you can transform your entire experience.

Let's take that same scenario and apply a pivot. Instead of fixating on the frustration, you decide to shift your thoughts: "I'm grateful to have a vehicle that gets me where I need to go. This traffic is giving me the opportunity to listen to some uplifting music or an inspiring podcast that I've been meaning to catch up on." What's happening here? You've taken control of your internal dialogue and redirected it from a place of negativity to a place of gratitude. This simple shift in perspective doesn't just alter your thoughts; it changes the energy you bring to the situation, transforming your emotional experience in the process.

I can tell you this from personal experience—I used to allow minor inconveniences like traffic to dictate my mood for the entire day. The frustration would spill over into everything I did, making me irritable and draining my energy. But when I started practicing the art of the pivot, something remarkable happened. The traffic didn't change, but I did. Instead of arriving at my destination stressed and worn out, I found myself feeling calm, centered, and even grateful. I began to enjoy these once-dreaded moments, using them as opportunities to nurture my mind and spirit.

This is the transformative power of language. When you learn to pivot your thoughts and words, you're not just changing your mindset—you're shifting your entire vibrational energy. And when your energy shifts, your experience of life shifts with it. The situations may remain the same, but your response—and therefore your reality—becomes one of peace, gratitude, and empowerment.

Becoming Your Own Best Friend: The Power of Self-Compassion

Imagine this: Your best friend is going through a tough time. Maybe they've made a mistake at work or are feeling overwhelmed by a major life decision. Without hesitation, you offer them words of comfort and encouragement. You remind them of their strengths, their past successes, and assure them that this too shall pass. You see their potential clearly, even when they don't. Now, what if you could offer that same level of support and kindness to yourself?

This is where the concept of becoming your own best friend comes into play. It's about shifting the way you speak to yourself, especially during moments of doubt or hardship. Too often, we reserve our kindness and understanding for others, while treating ourselves with harshness and criticism. We become our own worst enemy, scrutinizing every mistake and questioning our worth. But what if, instead, we chose to be our own greatest ally?

When you're faced with a difficult choice or when life feels overwhelming, pause and ask yourself: "What would I say to my best friend in this situation?" You would likely offer them a perspective that's both compassionate and constructive. You would acknowledge their feelings without judgment and encourage them to see the bigger picture. Now, try applying that same approach to yourself.

For example, let's say you're struggling with a decision about whether to pursue a new career path. Fear and doubt might start creeping in, telling you that you're not good enough or that you'll fail. But if your best friend came to you with the same fears, how would you respond? You'd probably remind them of their skills, their past accomplishments, and the potential for growth that lies ahead. You'd help them see the situation through a lens of possibility rather than limitation.

By becoming your own best friend, you start to cultivate an inner dialogue that's supportive and empowering. You learn to treat yourself with the same level of compassion and understanding that you so freely give to others. This doesn't mean ignoring your challenges or brushing aside your emotions. Instead, it's about acknowledging them and choosing to respond with kindness, knowing that you deserve the same love and respect that you offer to the people you care about.

In my own journey, I found that this shift was transformative. I used to be my own harshest critic, constantly doubting my abilities and fearing failure. But when I started treating myself as I would my best friend, everything changed. I began to approach challenges with a sense of calm and clarity, and I was able to make decisions from a place of confidence rather than fear.

Think of the times when you've been there for a friend during their toughest moments. The care, patience, and encouragement you offered made a difference in their life. Now, imagine the impact of turning that same energy inward. When you become your own best friend, you create a foundation of self-love and trust that can carry you through life's inevitable ups and downs. You empower yourself to navigate challenges with grace and to celebrate your victories, no matter how small.

This practice of self-compassion is not just a feel-good exercise—it's a powerful tool for personal growth. It allows you to build a strong, supportive relationship with yourself, which is essential for manifesting the life you desire. After all, if you can't be kind to yourself, how can you expect to attract kindness from the universe?

So the next time you find yourself in a difficult situation, take a step back and ask, "What would I say to my best friend right now?" Then, turn those words inward. Offer yourself the same compassion, wisdom, and encouragement. By doing so, you'll find that you're not just surviving life's challenges—you're thriving through them.

The Power of Gratitude

Gratitude has been nothing short of transformative in my journey toward elevating my thoughts, energy, and overall life experience. It's more than just saying "thank you"—it's about recognizing and deeply appreciating the abundance that already exists in your life. When you make a conscious effort to acknowledge even the smallest blessings, you begin to shift your perspective. This shift is not just mental; it resonates on an energetic level, aligning you with the universe's natural flow of abundance.

Imagine waking up each day and instead of rushing into the stresses of the day, you take a moment to appreciate the warmth of the morning sun, the comfort of your bed, or the fresh air filling your lungs. These are simple yet profound moments of gratitude. When you practice this consistently, something magical happens—you start vibrating at a higher frequency. This elevated vibrational state isn't just a feel-good experience; it sends a powerful signal to the universe that you are open to receiving better in your life.

Gratitude serves as a magnet, attracting more of what you are thankful for. When you consciously focus on what you already have, your mind and heart open up to even greater possibilities. You teach your subconscious mind to expect and accept the best, rather than dwelling on what is lacking. This mindset shift is crucial because it changes how you interact with the world. Instead of approaching life from a place of scarcity or fear, you start operating from a place of abundance and trust.

In my own life, I noticed a profound difference when I began integrating a daily gratitude practice. It wasn't just about feeling good in the moment; it was about rewiring my entire thought process. I made it a point to keep my goals at the forefront of my mind, but instead of stressing over them, I paired them with a sense of gratitude. I began to thank the universe for the opportunities that hadn't yet arrived, but that I believed were on their way. This practice did more than just elevate my mood—it aligned my energy with my highest intentions.

The results were undeniable. As I maintained this practice, the universe responded in kind. Opportunities began to appear, often in unexpected ways. People, resources, and situations that supported my goals started to show up in my life, as if drawn to my elevated energy. This wasn't a coincidence—it was the universe conspiring to support my intentions.

As Ralph Waldo Emerson wisely said, *"Once you make a decision, the universe conspires to make it happen."*

To put it simply, shifting and rewiring your mindset through a consistent gratitude practice is one of the quickest and most effective ways to elevate your thoughts daily. It's a powerful tool that not only changes your outlook but also your reality. When you elevate your emotions through positive thoughts and gratitude, you raise your vibrational frequency. This higher frequency is in harmony with the universe's highest power, enabling you to attract and manifest your desired results with greater ease and clarity.

Gratitude is more than just a practice—it's a way of life. It's a commitment to seeing the world through a lens of abundance and positivity. When you make gratitude a cornerstone of your daily routine, you create a solid foundation for a life filled with joy, fulfillment, and endless possibilities.

Tools for Transformation: Affirmations and Visualization

To truly harness the universe's highest energy and align yourself with your deepest desires, I turned to two powerful and transformative tools: Affirmations and Visualization. These tools have the potential to accelerate your journey toward your goals by fundamentally shifting your mindset and energy.

Affirmations are not just positive statements; they are declarations of your desired reality, spoken in the present tense as if they have already come true. The magic of affirmations lies in their ability to reprogram your subconscious mind, shaping your beliefs and behaviors to match your goals. But here's the key: affirmations must be infused with genuine emotion. The more you feel the truth of these statements, the more powerfully they resonate within you.

For example, if your goal is to achieve optimal health, you might affirm, "I am thrilled to have a vibrant, healthy body." Notice the specificity and the emotion in this affirmation—it's not just a neutral statement; it's a joyful declaration of your desired state. The words we speak carry immense power because they shape our inner reality. Every word you utter is a command to your subconscious mind, which then works tirelessly to align your outer world with these inner declarations.

Consider the impact of negative self-talk: if you find yourself saying, "Why can't I be successful?" your brain focuses on the word "can't." This seemingly innocent question becomes a self-fulfilling prophecy, as your subconscious mind begins to manifest obstacles that prevent success. This is why it's crucial to be mindful of the language you use—every thought, every word is an instruction to your inner self, setting the stage for your future experiences.

To begin transforming your reality, start with a few affirmations tailored specifically to your goals. You don't need a long list; four or five well-chosen affirmations are more than enough to start with. These statements should be simple, direct, and emotionally charged. Here are some examples from my personal list that have profoundly impacted my life:

ALL IS GOOD

- EVERYTHING IS WORKING OUT FOR MY HIGHEST GOOD.

- **OUT OF EVERY SITUATION OR EXPERIENCE, ONLY GOOD WILL COME TO ME.**

- **I AM GRATEFUL THAT I AM SAFE AND PROTECTED.**

- **I AM GRATEFUL THAT I AM HAPPY AND ALWAYS LOVED.**

These affirmations are not just words; they are a daily practice that elevates my energy and shifts my thought patterns. By repeating these statements with conviction, I began to notice a shift in my emotional state and, subsequently, in my external reality. My days became filled with more positivity, resilience, and alignment with my true desires.

Visualization takes the power of affirmations a step further. It's the practice of creating a vivid mental image of your affirmations, turning them into a "mind movie" where you see, feel, and experience your desires as if they have already manifested. Visualization isn't just about seeing an image in your mind—it's about immersing yourself in the emotions associated with that image. When you visualize your goals, you are essentially training your mind to recognize and create the reality you desire.

Every day, I dedicated a few minutes to this practice. I would close my eyes, take a few deep breaths, and imagine my affirmations as if they had already come to pass. I saw myself living the life I desired, feeling the joy, peace, and fulfilment that came with it. The more detailed and emotionally charged the visualization, the more real it became in my mind.

I began and ended each day with specific affirmations and visualization, surrendering to the universe to bring me my desires or something even better. This practice became a sacred ritual, especially during the early morning and before bed—time when the subconscious mind is most receptive. During these moments, your mind is in a more relaxed, meditative state, allowing your visualizations and affirmations to penetrate deeply, laying the groundwork for your future experiences.

The changes I witnessed were nothing short of miraculous. Opportunities began to appear, relationships flourished, and I felt a sense of inner peace that I had never experienced before. By committing to this daily practice, I not only shifted my mindset but also my entire life trajectory.

In essence, these tools—affirmations and visualization—are your keys to becoming a powerful **MANIFESTOR.** When you consistently affirm and visualize your goals with elevated emotions, you align yourself with the universe's highest energy. This alignment allows you to effortlessly attract and manifest the life you truly desire.

Remember, the universe is always listening, responding to the energy you put out. By consciously choosing your words and images, you take an active role in shaping your destiny. The power is within you—*ask for what you desire, believe in its possibility, take inspired action, and remain open to receiving it in ways you might never have imagined.* This is how you unlock the universe's full potential and bring your dreams to life.

Becoming a Manifestor: Unlocking Your Creative Power

Imagine having the ability to shape your reality, to turn your deepest desires into tangible outcomes. This is the essence of becoming a Manifestor—a person who not only dreams but also actively brings those dreams to life. It's about taking control of your destiny, rather than passively letting life happen to you.

The journey to becoming a Manifestor begins with a powerful combination of affirmations and visualization, but it doesn't stop there. As you consistently practice these tools, you'll start to notice subtle shifts in your life. Doors that were once closed will begin to open, opportunities will present themselves, and the right people will appear at the right time. This is no coincidence; it's the universe responding to the vibrational energy you're putting out.

But here's the key: when these opportunities arise, you must be ready to recognize them and take swift ACTION. The universe can only do so much. It can present you with the path, but it's up to you to walk it. This is where many people falter—they hesitate, overthink, or let fear hold them back. To become a true Manifestor, you must trust in the process, act with confidence, and seize the opportunities as they come.

Let's break down the process with the formula ASK – BELIEVE – ACT – RECEIVE:

1. **ASK:** The first step is to clearly ask the universe for what you desire. This isn't about simply wishing or hoping—it's about setting a clear, specific intention. Think of it as placing an order with the universe. You wouldn't go to a restaurant and tell the waiter to bring

you "whatever." You'd be specific, right? The same goes for manifesting. Be clear about what you want.

For example, if you desire a fulfilling career, don't just ask for "a good job." Instead, ask for a role that aligns with your passions, allows you to grow, and brings you joy and abundance.

2. **BELIEVE**: Once you've asked, the next step is to believe that what you desire is not only possible but inevitable. This belief must be unwavering. You must see your goal as something that's already on its way to you, even if you can't see it yet. This is where affirmations and visualization come into play. By repeatedly affirming your desires and visualizing them as already achieved,

you strengthen your belief, embedding it deep into your subconscious mind.

For instance, if you're manifesting a new home, visualize yourself living in that home. See the details—the color of the walls, the layout of the rooms, the feeling of comfort and security. Believe with all your heart that this home is already yours.

3. **ACT**: This is where many people get stuck. They ask and believe, but they forget to act. Manifestation is not about sitting back and waiting for things to happen. It's about taking inspired action. This means being proactive, following the guidance of your intuition, and moving towards your goals with purpose. When you take action, you signal to the universe that you're serious

about your desires, and this accelerates the manifestation process.

Let's say you're manifesting a new career opportunity. Believing isn't enough—you need to polish your resume, network with professionals in your field, and apply for positions that excite you. Each step you take brings you closer to your goal.

4. **RECEIVE**: Finally, you must be open to receiving what you've asked for. This might sound simple, but it can be challenging. Sometimes, what we receive isn't exactly what we imagined—but it's what we need. Trust that the universe has your best interests at heart. When you receive, do so with gratitude, knowing that this is part of a bigger plan for your life.

For example, if you were hoping for a promotion but instead get offered a different position in another company, embrace it. It might be the universe guiding you towards an even better path than you had envisioned.

As you align your thoughts, emotions, and actions with this powerful formula, you unlock the full potential of the universe to bring your desires into reality. This is the magic of manifestation. By becoming a Manifestor, you're not just passively waiting for life to happen—you're actively creating it, shaping your destiny with every thought, word, and action.

When I first began practicing this formula, I was astounded by the results. Opportunities I never imagined started coming my way—unexpected collaborations, new friendships, and breakthroughs in my personal and professional life. I realized that when you elevate your thoughts and emotions to align with the highest power, the universe responds in kind, conspiring to make your dreams come true.

By embracing your role as a Manifestor, you're taking the reins of your life, turning dreams into reality, and stepping into a life of purpose, abundance, and joy. The universe is ready to support you—are you ready to take action and receive its blessings?

◆ ◆ ◆

CONCLUSION

How many of you believe that living life consciously is not just important, but essential? How many of you desire a life filled with abundant health, wealth, fulfilling relationships, and a thriving career? And how many of you recognize that by vibrating at a higher frequency, you have the power to shift all the challenges in your life?

You hold the key to your future. Imagine where you want to be 5 or 10 years from now. Picture yourself living a life that's genuinely magical, where you're manifesting everything, you've ever desired.

The secret is simple: consistently vibrate at a higher frequency to align yourself with the energy of the universe. When you do this, the law of attraction begins to work in your favor.

The universe will send you opportunities—don't let them pass you by. These opportunities are signals, guiding you toward your destiny. Act on them with urgency and trust the process.

Remember, this is just the beginning of your journey. The universe is always supporting you. By putting the right thoughts into your mind, elevating your emotions, and raising your vibrational frequency, you'll achieve the results you desire and live the life of your dreams.

The power is within you. Now, it's time to harness it.

Join me, Vinti Bharati, on this transformative journey.

Follow me on Instagram @vinti_bharati or on www.vintibharat.com for one to one interaction by sending a direct message or follow me for daily inspirational insights that will keep you aligned with the life you desire.

◆ ◆ ◆

"ALL OUR DREAM
CAN COME TRUE
IF WE HAVE THE
CORAGE TO
PURSE THEM."

-WALT DISNEY

VINTI BHARATI

Before embarking on her transformative journey as a Life Transformational & Mindset Coach, Vinti Bharati faced a period of profound confusion and uncertainty about her life's direction. Driven by immense courage and a desire for change, she embarked on a journey of self-discovery, taking control of her inner world. As she began to transform internally, her external reality followed suit, shifting in remarkable ways.

Vinti struggled with self-identity, self-respect, and financial independence. However, her commitment to growth led her to extraordinary learning opportunities. Under the guidance of esteemed mentors from around the world, she delved into life coaching, NLP, CBT, manifestation techniques, clearing block strategies, and the Law of Attraction. Her educational background in marketing and PR paved the way for her initial career as an Image Consultant, which eventually led her to become a Life Coach. Today, she empowers individuals to design and live their dream lives.

Her journey has been marked by significant achievements. As the President of WICCI for Karnataka, she empowered countless women, and in 2022, she was honoured by Femina as one of the top 8 women to inspire. In 2023, she received the Social Entrepreneur of the Year award from the Women Leaders Forum and set an Asia Book of Records for Inspiration with Success Gyan.

Through her coaching, she has helped thousands achieve a harmonious blend of personality and psychology, elevating their mindset to align with their true potential and manifest their desires.

Vinti's tools and insights into the Law of Attraction have proven transformative, enabling her clients to achieve remarkable results. Her work reflects her commitment to helping others live their dreams, driven by a deep understanding of global research and the wisdom gained from her mentors.

Vinti Bharati's Mantra Is Clear!!

"LIFE IS NOT WHAT HAPPENS TO US BUT HOW WE ASPIRE IT TO BE."